When There Is Little Light Left in Late Afternoon

When There Is Little Light Left in Late Afternoon

Poems by

Susan Oleferuk

Cover design by Shay Culligan

ISBN: 978-1-63980-142-8

Kelsay Books
502 South 1040 East, A-119
American Fork, Utah 84003
Kelsaybooks.com

To B, in all times

Acknowledgments

The Avocet: "Fairy Tale Summer," "Incident in the Woods," "Listening," "Waiting for Orpheus," "When a Tree Falls in the Woods," "When There is Little Light Left in the Late Afternoon"

The Deronda Review: "A Little Light," "Fairy Tale Summer," "In the Stillness," "Listening," "No Sky," "Quick Time," "The Smell of Snow," "The Tree Arm Tapped," "This Hour in Summer," "Waiting for Orpheus," "When a Tree Falls in the Woods," "Where Do the Swallows Go"

The Weekly Avocet: "NoSky," "The Smell of Snow," "This Hour in Summer," "When There is Little Light Left in the Late Afternoon," "Where Do the Swallows Go"

Contents

When There Is Little Light Left in Late Afternoon

When there is little light left in late afternoon
and the autumnal clouds start chilling the sky
living creatures find their way home
and I search above and below with my eye
for one small place I know my own
to remember in case I must go
so I can say I saw great beauty in the dim
and moments of glory in the ending glow.

No Sky

I didn't see the sky today
I didn't see its light rise in the east like a great beast
or shred its past in restless white tatters and then hurry on
I didn't see the sky today
when the flurries were strewn
wrapped gifts each holding itself in soft down
I did not see the sky slowly pace into night
and open a door to maps of chalkboard with prophecies written and
love aligned
for today there was no space or time
a day ground down to heartless dust
a day not mine.

When a Tree Falls in the Woods

What happens when a tree falls in the woods
sound or no sound
after the storm I walk the trail
it is a woesome thing, a dead thing so grand it knew the sky
its leaves still green with summer's soft hand
its roots ripped out of the earth like a heart missing a dream
its trunk wanton, wayward and wrong
still a natural death
the bark, roots, leaves and wood go to the groundand
I will say a prayer and mourn
and that is the sound.

The Smell of Snow

The sun was leaving as we left the river
the wind slapping and pushing
to climb a trail steep, frail thin as if it would snap
the wind in an angry fit kicking the leaves back and forth
the coyote in its steel winter gray on a distant hill watching us
its eyes like the bores of a gun

We stopped to watch the shadow creep across the hill
and smell the coming snow
the smell that holds all the magical elements of earth and sky
that make you feel the mountain and rock are your very bones
nearby a little house nestled bright and warm
and we wondered which really was our home.

Incident in the Woods

I saw the hawk that had killed the goldfinch
no sentimentality here
no hawk placed snugly on one's arm
to stroke, soothe, seduce
no goldfinch like the sun itself chained inside a house
No, on the path
the hawk must have swept down like an old god of war
and the pretty victim shook
no morality here
I saw the hawk that had killed the goldfinch
I wondered which one I would want to be
then realized both belonged in a mind far from mine
a sky and treetops I would never see
I took one feather
the others would carry the tale of the death far
and I was but one small part of the story.

Listening

I know a tree
it stands hidden high on a hill of the Hudson Highlands
the tree has a bole, a hole
just my height
a big round "O" like from a child's crayon

The tree is the only elder I still have living
so I talk to it
it listens
it listens well
I have spent my grown years listening too
 but never did I leave anyone breathing cool air,
gazing at the tender river supine below and taking off friskily
down a path

When I pass, I'd like to turn into a leaf
on the tallest branch of my friend tree
so I can see so far into the world too
and counsel wayfarers so wisely.

In the Stillness

In the stillness of the summer afternoon
the bees hum the loneliness of the hours
and you wonder if you will ever gather the flowers again
if second chances will be brought by a wind

In the stillness of long Sundays
baked in sun and steamed in smells
with children bored and red
you wonder why and you wonder when

In the stillness of the soreness
after the betrayal has fallen like sickness
your heart sounds like steps running away
you wonder if you will follow after

Night's stillness is its own with black folds
pressing against the forehead like an effigy crowned
stalking dread and worry
mighty night of sneaky sound

Come sit still a bit and let your heartbeat echo far
off the mountains, trees, sea and moving tide
come bellow, hoot, buzz and roar
to this magnificent moonsoaked earth.

This Hour in Summer

White lilies lean over the soft dark grass of a summer evening
glows and hums unsettling
in this hour, in this only hour
all whispering of love and loss and desire
swift and strange as fairy lights
translucent and vertiginous the milky swarm of stars
the purplish shadows of the past lurking through the trees
spilling like a dark hood
this hour gives one more moment with the moon lending her light
and the ghostly forms of flowers close their mouths and bend and
pray
in the crying mists
and creatures fly their fantastic ways
and we leave to restless lives
such is this hour
if you follow it
in summer.

The Tree Arm Tapped

The tree arm tapped for me
to come, see, smell, sit, climb
walk under it properly
the pine outside
season after season
a window between
a dry office and a drenching green
and I declined

Love, life is hard to find
one must look behind
lift the leaf, rub the knobs, grasp for
that shaking branch
study the hard ridges like standing armies
sneak on pass
trace the root, scan the heights
lean against it
step outside.

Fairy Tale Summer

When the cottonwood flies like white
wishesflicked from a wand
and the chorus is loud
from green princelings parading
intheir kingdom of Pond
and birds eggs broken bright blue in needles of
pineare treasures to find
summer's magic is borne on the lights of fireflies

Mother moon will bathe all who wish to wash
in her silvery rivers with scents sultry
and pushing deep into knowing
hiddensand tempting shadowy walks
forbiddenAll is soft, all is hard, all is
forgiven stand on one foot and dance
to remember the
landwe once lived
in.

Magic Isle

The clump of reeds drifted on the pond
making an island
an Avalon
for those who dreamed
landless but with roots reaching deep
it drifted
till my inquisitive companion dove and visited
a noble princess wearing a filigree of green slime
my enchanted dog
always bringing me
what I left behind.

Quick Time

I have a moment
I took a moment though I don't know who I took it from
I spent days in coins, dollars
time, it is said, is money
yet I lack both
I once slept years like Sleeping Beauty
I'm awake now
I can't say for how long
Time is on your side
I am on no one's side
I hate to see anyone lose
can't we call it even

This will take a moment to finish
I'm filling in the moment like a coloring book
It's an afternoon in June and I'm sitting under a cascade of pink
roses
my black dog is at my feet
the honeysuckle on the breeze is sweet
my dog ran hard and I fought to stay alive
and that is our whole life story.

Waiting for Orpheus

Loneliness smothers soft
  a shawl, a shell of window glass
  a few steps here and there
  to the chair
  and it grows in the night
  mold leaving a dullness century old on shoes and eyes
  in the afternoon hours
  a hole

There are silhouettes of trees blackened on the hills under dark
  skies
  skeletal buildings sagging over a tired river
  cement plants holding out lost arms
  I am patterned here, placed as firmly as the concrete blocks
  molded in the clay and rubble where stunted sumac fights for its
  share
  I am waiting for Orpheus
  sleek and brown
  I met him once
  when I was young.

Every Summer

The leaves' trembling
can't hold a summer's day
with shadows stalking from the cover of stone walls
then sliding under the watchful pines
to pool in mysterious ponderance

This mantle of sun warmth
invincible for a day, at peace for a day
near water expanding like a lily pad
into colors blue, green and gray and silver fish flashing
and scents that stir the colors into spells

One cannot hold a summers day
too bright to be browned by sad memory
brief summer, every summer
 in the chart of the gracious sun and tempting licking moonlight
be as one.

Where Do the Swallows Go

Where do the swallows go so fast
in the slow summer evenings
when the trees start rippling
shaking my heart back to fluttering life
the swallows
scrolling epiphanies in air
where do they go so fast
to a tree they chose as a home for the night

I walk the well-worn steps
and at my door turn back and ask
where can I walk so fast
to a chosen tree for the night
to be a pilgrim under the sky
send a soft sound
make a movement of heartbreak
and make the earth my home.

Closed

When the earth closes, it crusts and eats
itself away in dust
the rain cannot enter, but hits hard
slashing insults
while water drains away in brooding ponding to linger
and murmur rumors of lessening and longing.

The flowers don't close nor leaf or bud
or expanse of tree crest
nothing that desires warmth from the sun
and wants to flash colors and body
from sky to earth in an ecstasy of the winds and lightening
of its creation

The rock humble, dull and grave
over the years splits and makes a grin
and in come the crawlers and creepers and mosses
soft footed all cradled in a hard mouth
that spits small spirits
back into earth and capricious air

We, we close like a scowly night
dance under moon's false light
reflect ourselves and our enlarged shadows
 colorless
slim silhouettes
hiding in the darkness of closed fear.

The Dimensions of Time

I place my hand on the inside of the bark
of the broken tree
it is smooth with written runes
tree history the dimension of the past
this history true
for who could doubt the integrity of a tree
time is curved like a treetop
past, present and the future
then there is the dimension of regret
distortion
omission
so many dimensions of the past
while the present is a block of bullet lists busy
and the future in the loss of the curves of trees
and thus the dimension of hope and wide open joy
the art of a leaf and the holding of a chestnut handsome skinned
in human time the dimension of seasons
parallel to the curve of our years
and when I too break under the years, I will wonder
what the runes meant.

Middletown

In a town you don't know
halfway between one place
and where you want to go
you find yourself sitting on the curb of an off lane road
waiting on a cloud filled summer day
the storming of a lawn mower a few blocks away
suspended in the heavy air and holding nothing but waiting time
like you are splayed and still in amber
forced to watch the bee in the bush and your own shoes
and wonder if you can live on this street
who lives here with no one around
but a cat edging a building's walls
in this small town with cars passing here and there
and in your farthest mind
you've never sat so alone.

A Little Light

Roof to roof
lines sharp slope
chimneys faint smoke
who sleeps under these roofs
friend or foe maybe awake too
or dreaming their dreams as selfsame
as the crescents, circuits, swirls, secrets
of their fingers
a light left somewhere
the ancient fire, candle, heart of home hearth
a little light to fight the dark
light to light
star to star over
roof to roof.

About the Author

Susan Oleferuk is the author of *Circling for Home, Those Who Come to the Garden* and *Days of Sun,* all published by Finishing Line Press. She teaches in colleges in and around New York City.

www.ingramcontent.com/pod-product-compliance
Lightning Source LLC
Chambersburg PA
CBHW031156090426
42738CB00008B/1355